In the Sky

Adria F. Klein

DOMINIE PRESS
Pearson Learning Group

Publisher: Christine Yuen
Series Editors: Adria F. Klein & Alan Trussell-Cullen
Editors: Bob Rowland & Paige Sanderson
Designers: Gary Hamada & Lois Stanfield
Photographer: Aaron Scholl

Copyright ©2001 Dominie Press, Inc. All rights reserved. No part of this publication may be reproduced or transmitted in any form or by any means without permission in writing from the publisher. Reproduction of any part of this book, through photocopy, recording, or any electronic or mechanical retrieval system, without the written permission of the publisher, is an infringement of the copyright law.

Published by:

Dominie Press, Inc.

1949 Kellogg Avenue
Carlsbad, California 92008 USA

www.dominie.com

ISBN 0-7685-1511-4

Printed in Singapore by PH Productions Pte Ltd

6 7 8 9 10   10 09 08

Table of Contents

I See the Sun   4

I See the Stars   6

I See the Moon   8

I See Many Objects in the Sky   10

Picture Glossary   11

Index   12

I like to look at the sky.
I see the Sun in the sky.
But I should never look into the Sun.

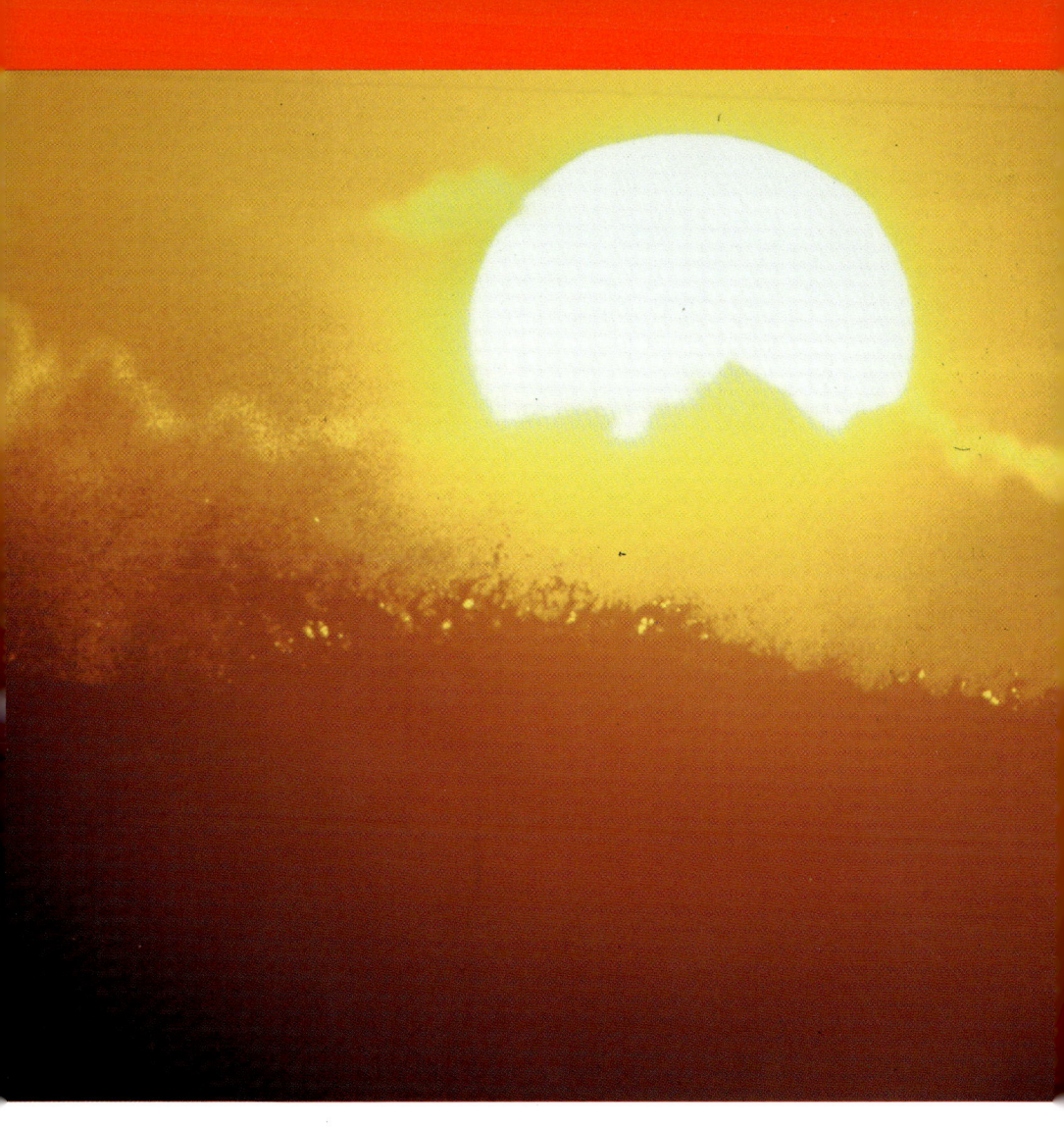

The sun is big and bright.
It shines in the daytime.

I like to look at the sky.
I see many stars in the sky.

They are little and bright.
They shine in the nighttime.

I like to look at the sky.
I see the Moon in the sky.

8

Sometimes the Moon is little.
Sometimes the Moon is big.
It is always bright.
It shines in the nighttime.

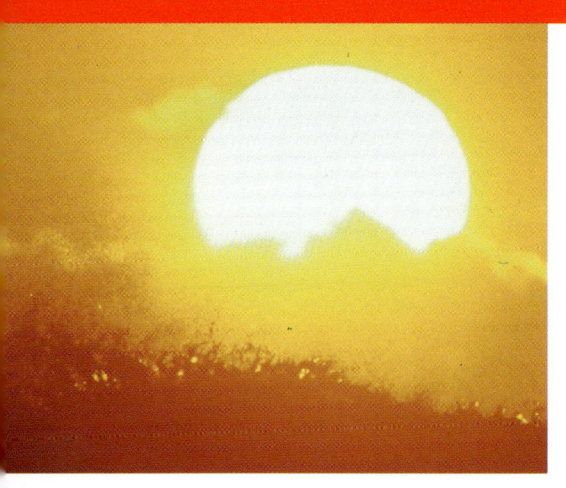

I like to look at the sky.
I see the Sun in the daytime.
I see the stars and the Moon in the nighttime.
I see many objects in the sky.

Picture Glossary

Moon:

stars:

sky:

Sun:

11

Index

Moon,   8, 9, 10

sky,   4, 6, 8, 10
stars,   6, 10
Sun,   4, 5, 10